Young Riders Guides

Riding and Schooling

This book is intended for people who have already mastered the basic skills of riding and who would like to improve their own and their ponies' performance and get the most out of their riding in every way. The authors describe the importance of a good seat and hands, and give valuable advice on the natural and artificial aids and finer points of schooling. There is a section on going for a ride, advice on the correct dress, and finally a useful glossary of terms.

The two previous books in the series, *Buying and Keeping a Horse or Pony* and *Caring for a Horse or Pony*, were described in *Horse and Hound* as 'packed with useful information, well presented and easily assimilated', and *Riding and Schooling* will be a valuable addition to the bookshelf of any enthusiastic young rider.

Young Riders Guides
Riding and Schooling

Robert Owen and John Bullock

*Illustrated by James Val and
Peter Kesteven*

Beaver Books

First published in 1977 by
The Hamlyn Publishing Group Limited
London · New York · Sydney · Toronto
Astronaut House, Feltham, Middlesex, England

© Copyright Text Robert Owen/John Bullock 1977
© Copyright Line illustrations
The Hamlyn Publishing Group Limited 1977
ISBN 0 600 37582 X

Printed in England by
Cox and Wyman Limited, London, Reading and Fakenham
Set in Monotype Univers
Cover artwork by Gwen Green

Contents

Going for a ride

The correct dress

Glossary 76

Introduction

There is more to riding than just sitting midway between a horse's head and his tail. It is an art which can give enormous pleasure, but like all sports, there is a correct way of doing everything.

In this book we have not set out to teach you to ride. That is the job of an experienced instructor who can correct your faults as you go along, and who can see whether you have reached the stage when you are perhaps trying to exceed your own capabilities or those of your horse or pony.

Our object is to encourage those of you who have started riding, or indeed who may by now be quite experienced, to take a closer look at how you are riding. Have you got into bad habits without realising it? Are you perhaps doing something incorrectly, because you have never really understood the reasons why one way is correct and the other is wrong? Are you getting all the pleasure you can out of your riding, or would you get more enjoyment if you had a little more help in understanding some of the finer points? Would you just like to improve your riding and your knowledge of horses?

If the answer to any of these questions is 'yes' then we hope you will enjoy this book.

R.O.
J.B.

Acknowledgements

The photographs in this book were supplied by the following:

The British Tourist Authority: plate 9
Photonews: plate 2
Equestrian (Press and General) Services Limited: back cover;
plates 1, 3, 4, 5, 6, 7, 8, 10, 11
The Wales Tourist Board: front cover

The importance of hands and seat

What is the correct way to mount?

Before mounting make sure that the girth is tight enough to prevent the saddle from slipping, and that both stirrup irons are down. The leathers should also be approximately the correct length, and this can be checked by seeing whether they are the same length as your arm from the tips of the fingers to the armpit.

To mount, stand on the near side of the horse, facing the tail, at right angles to the point of the shoulder, and take the reins and stick in the left hand. The reins should be separated ready for riding with the off-side rein slightly shorter than the near, so that should your horse move, his quarters will swing towards you. Both reins, however, should be short enough to control the horse or pony properly if he does try to move forward.

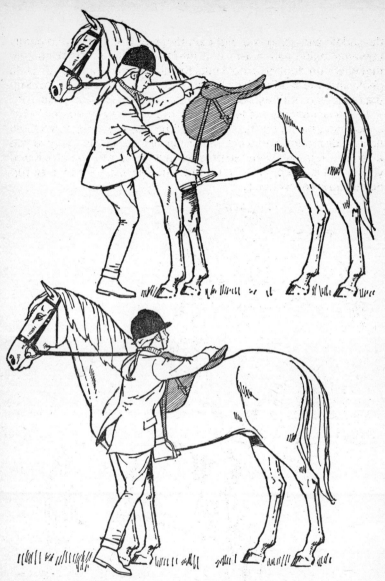

Place the left hand in front of the withers and, holding the stirrup leather with the right hand, put your left foot into the stirrup with the leather twisted round clockwise. Press the toe down under the girth, then, moving your right hand on to the middle of the saddle and using your right leg rather as a spring, swing gently upwards taking care not to flop into the saddle, and making sure that your right foot does not strike the horse's quarters. As you slide gently into the saddle, place the right foot in the stirrup, and take up the reins with both hands ready to move off. (See also plate 1.)

It is most important to learn to mount correctly without the aid of a mounting block, because there will be occasions when you will have to dismount, and there will not be anyone around to give you a 'leg up'. It is also useful to practice mounting from the off-side. If your horse is too high for you to mount easily, then let the stirrup leather down a few holes.

And to dismount?

When the time comes to dismount, remove both feet from the stirrups and leaning forward place your left hand, which should be holding the stick and reins, on the horse's neck. Then vault off by placing the right hand on the pommel of the saddle, and making sure that your right leg is well clear of the horse's quarters, land gently on your toes, facing the saddle, and well clear of the horse's legs. You can then take a firm hold of the reins close to the bit with your right hand.

Never dismount by throwing your right leg over the horse's withers. It may look clever but in doing so you would have to drop the reins and your control of the horse would be lost, particularly if anything caused him to shy.

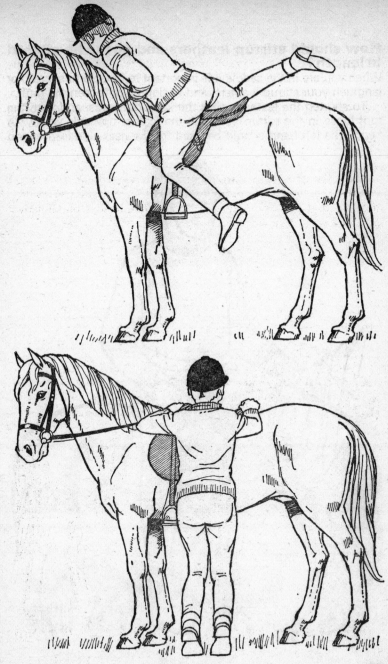

How should stirrup leathers and girths be altered in length?

When you are in the saddle it is important to be able to shorten or lengthen your stirrup leathers, and to tighten or loosen the girth.

To shorten the leathers, shift the knee outwards, and with the foot loose in the stirrup iron, pull the leather upwards with your hand. The left hand should be used for the near-side leather and

the right hand for the off-side. When the leather is loose feel with your hand for the correct hole, and then run the buckle up to it and make it secure in the stirrup bar by pressing your foot down in the stirrup iron. Never drop the reins and fumble about with both hands, because this would mean you would lose control, and if your horse became frightened you could quickly find yourself in trouble. Practice will enable you to alter stirrup lengths quickly by feel without looking down, but always remember that your feet should never be removed from the stirrups when you are doing so.

Loosening or tightening the girths can also be done very easily from the saddle. Lift your leg forward on the side that you intend to alter the girth length, and lifting the saddle flap with your hand, take a firm hold of the girth strap. Having freed the buckle you will be able to loosen or tighten the girth as required. By keeping your first finger on the point of the buckle as you do so you can then press the point safely home into the correct hole.

How should the reins be held and shortened?

Although the reins should be held in both hands, there are several methods of doing so, and there will also be occasions when it will be necessary to hold both reins in one hand, as for example when mounting and dismounting.

Holding a snaffle rein in one hand

The picture shows the correct position of the hands when holding a plain snaffle. The backs of the hands are turned out and the hands are held comfortably just above the withers.

The backs of the hands must always be turned outwards, and with a bit where only one rein is used, like with a plain snaffle or a kimblewick, the easiest way is to pick up the reins, placing them outside the little finger and bringing them up through the palms of the hands. Some people prefer to place them between the little and third finger and then bring them up in the same way.

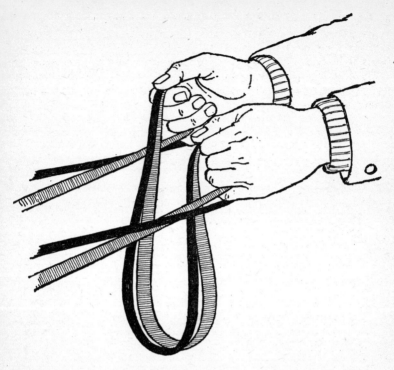

The correct way of holding the reins used with a double bridle or pelham. The thinner rein (black in the picture) is the bridoon or snaffle-rein and the broader rein is the curb rein.

With all bridles which have two reins, like a double bridle or a pelham, the curb rein should be picked up inside the little finger with the third finger in between. Do this with both hands, and then take up the snaffle-rein or bridoon and place it outside the little finger.

Always remember that the reins should be brought through the fingers to the correct length and then held firmly by the thumb.

When shortening the reins, one hand should slide down the reins, letting the other take up the slack.

Remember the influence of the seat is of paramount importance when the reins are being used. The whole body must act in concerted action, and it is no good expecting to get good results by just using the hands alone.

What is meant by a good seat?

A good seat depends on a combination of balance, suppleness and grip, and when people refer to 'the seat' they really mean the position in the saddle and the control the rider has over the horse.

By riding regularly you will be able to acquire and maintain a good, strong seat, and be independent of any need for assistance from the reins.

A good seat

How should the rider sit ?

Although people talk of the 'correct seat' it is more important for a rider to develop a comfortable and relaxed seat, so that the movements of the horse can be followed without strain, and what is equally important, the horse will also be comfortable and at ease.

If a horse throws his head up, it is usually because he has been jerked in the mouth; if he swishes his tail it may mean that the rider's legs are fidgeting, or if he raises his hindquarters it could be because the rider is sitting too far back.

The horse's centre of gravity runs along a vertical line passing through the withers, so that the closer you sit to the pommel of your saddle the less you will feel the movement of the horse's

This rider's seat shows several bad faults. Instead of sitting upright and maintaining light contact with his pony's mouth he is leaning back and using the reins to hold on with. His stirrup leathers are too long so that his toes point downwards instead of slightly up. Both rider and pony look very uncomfortable and he has no control. Compare this with the picture opposite.

Here the pony and rider are relaxed and in harmony. The rider is sitting naturally upright with shoulders square and her back straight. Her lower leg is slightly back and the heel just below the level of the toe. The stirrup iron is under the ball of her foot and the foot points forwards. Her forearms and the reins make a straight line through to the pony's mouth for good contact and control.

paces or gaits, and the easier it will be for you to 'go with' your horse.

One of the chief faults is sitting with a 'hollow' back, which makes it difficult for the rider to sit deep enough in the saddle. The upper part of the body should be upright, but free from all stiffness, particularly about the waist. Stiffness in one part of the body will make the muscles contract in another.

Make sure you do not stiffen up, but at the same time, sit up straight with your shoulders squared and your head erect, so that you can look between the horse's ears. Your knees and thighs should be close to the saddle, with the knees and ankles supple. If these joints become stiff the upper part of the body will also be stiff.

The lower part of the leg should be back slightly so that pressure can be applied behind the girth as and when required. A bad leg position will create bad balance.

The heels need to be kept below the level of the toes to ensure that the muscles on the inside of the thigh are kept taut, and the knee is as low as possible on the saddle.

The tread of the stirrup should be in line with your ankle when your feet are out of the stirrup irons and allowed to go limp. For most of the time the stirrups should be held on the ball of the foot. When the ball of your foot is in the iron the toes should be pointing upwards. They should also point towards the front, because if they are pointed outwards you will have a tendency to grip with the back of the calf.

Your arms should hang naturally down to the elbows and be kept close in to the sides; the elbows should be bent and the forearms should form a straight line through the reins to the horse's mouth. The hands, with the wrists flexible, should be held just above and in front of the front arch of the saddle, with the fingers closed over the reins thumbs uppermost.

Your position will be correct in the saddle when there is an imaginary line from your ears, over your shoulders and hips to your heels.

Although there are certain fundamental principles which should be followed, some riders like to ride with a short stirrup, while others prefer a medium or longer length of stirrup. It is up to you to decide which way you want to ride and then stick to it, so long as the horse is not caused any discomfort and you can maintain an easy, comfortable and graceful seat. A good position in the saddle will not only add to your grace as a rider, it will also add to your effectiveness when giving the aids.

What is meant by 'good hands'?

The reins help the rider to regulate the pace and direction of a horse, and to keep it properly balanced. The horse has to accept the bit and not to fight against it, but to hold it lightly in his mouth. For this reason it is important for a rider's hands to be light and responsive, and to be able to 'give' and 'take' according to the movement of the horse, rather like a reflex action.

A rider with light and sensitive hands will feel a horse beginning to resist before the resistance becomes obvious, and will quickly be able to take the necessary corrective action.

Although the use of the bit is of prior importance, a good rider always ensures that his hands are used in conjunction with the seat, back and legs. Incorrect use of the hands, however, can quickly mar a horse's mouth, making what is known as a 'hard mouth'.

The hands should remain just above and to each side of the withers, so that the reins make a straight line from the horse's mouth to the rider's elbows. They should remain steady and one hand should be used to 'ask' a horse for obedience, while the other should retain a light contact on the mouth. The hand doing the 'asking' should not be pulled backwards and forwards, but have an action rather like squeezing a sponge. As soon as the horse obeys the command by flexing his jaw, the hand can be relaxed again to retain a light contact with the mouth. If the horse shows any signs of further resistance, pressure can quickly be re-applied until the horse again obeys the rider's commands.

The forearms and wrists must be supple and act as a 'buffer' between the horse's mouth and the movement of the rider. An experienced horseman will sit erect and there will only be a minimum of movement of the hands.

Always remember that a horse's mouth is very sensitive, unless it has already been ruined by a heavy-handed rider, and if the hands are worked backwards and forwards, or up and down, with every movement of the rider's body, the poor horse will be continually getting a jab in the mouth until it becomes insensitive to the rider's commands.

A rider must aim at developing a strong independent seat as quickly as possible and not rely upon the reins in order to keep his position in the saddle. Good hands are not possible without a good strong seat.

Plate 3 shows a rider with excellent combination of hands and seat, so that the horse is alert and ready for the rider's commands.

In this picture the rider shows the necessity for good hands. The hands, just above and to each side of the withers, remain steady and in contact as the horse moves along. In conjunction with her firm relaxed seat this makes for maximum control and enjoyment for rider and horse.

The aids

What are the natural and artificial aids?

In riding the word 'aids' has two distinct meanings, depending on whether the rider is referring to the 'natural' aids or the 'artificial' aids.

The 'natural' aids are the signals used by a rider to convey his intentions to the horse, which the horse must learn to understand and obey. In doing this the rider uses his hands, legs, body and voice. The 'artificial' aids by which a rider can signal his intention to his horse are items such as whips, spurs and martingales. If, for example, a horse is being lunged, the trainer would use his voice as a 'natural' aid assisted by the 'artificial' aids of the cavesson and whip.

Lungeing is the method by which a horse is exercised, usually without anyone on his back, by means of a lunge rein held by the person exercising the horse, which is clipped to a ring attached to a cavesson head-collar. In response to the voice and the careful and skilful use of the whip, the horse is persuaded to walk, trot and canter in a circle round the instructor. Care, however, must be taken to ensure that the direction of the circle is changed at frequent intervals to prevent the possibility of the horse becoming one-sided. The picture on pages 26–7 shows a horse being lunged without a rider but saddled up.

Always remember when riding that the lightest possible aid should be used in order to get the best results. A young horse will need an exaggerated and more definite aid, but the aids given to a well-schooled horse should be hardly visible to the onlooker. Complete harmony of hands, legs and body will be needed, and artificial aids like the stick and spurs must be used sparingly.

Spurs are there, not as a means of punishing a horse, but to make him light and responsive to the leg. The inside of the spur should be used against the horse's sides, and care should be taken not to turn the toe outwards, resulting in the sharp end of the spur being used.

What is the action of the hands and legs?

The chief aids used to inform a horse of his rider's wishes are the hands and legs used in conjunction with the seat.

In simple language, the legs are used for impulsion, and the hands guide and control the impulsion according to the demands of the rider. Once you have made up your mind what you want to do next, you have to communicate this to the horse. Some people claim that the basic aid of all is the mind and the will of the rider. Emotions of any kind, especially fear and anger, are instantly communicated to the horse, and he will usually react in no uncertain fashion. It is certainly important for a rider always to show coolness, confidence and patience, in order to remain in charge of the situation.

The leg aids are applied to begin with by increasing the pressure of the calves. If further pressure is required, the heels can be drawn

The 'natural' aids are the legs, voice, body and hands, used to indicate to the horse what his rider wants him to do.

back slightly and pressed against the horse's sides. If the horse does not obey the stick can be used to reinforce the orders given by the legs.

The aids given by the legs are comparatively simple compared with those of the hands. Aids given by the hands in particular should be intermittent, so that they never exert a prolonged pull on a horse's mouth, but 'give and take'.

The application of the aids given by the hands should begin with the flexing of the fingers, then of the wrists. Remember that the hands act directly on the mouth to make a horse flex his jaw and bend his neck, to raise or lower his head, to stop, to rein back, or to change direction.

It should be understood that the general aim of all applications of the aids is to influence the position and action of the horse's hindquarters which provide the source of all movements.

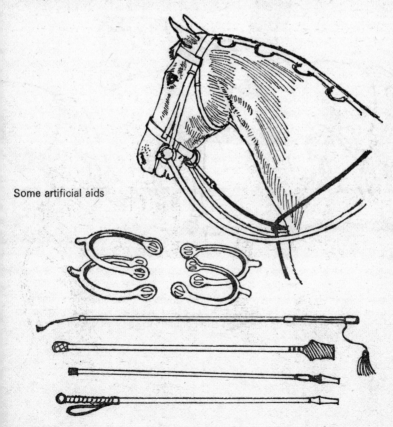

Some artificial aids

How can good changes of pace be achieved?

Once you have learnt to sit correctly and securely at the walk, trot, and canter, you must learn to control the change in pace smoothly and gracefully without any loss of rhythm.

Watch the movements of a horse running loose without a rider. He will change speed gracefully and with a minimum of fuss or excitement. If you can give the correct 'aids' to your horse quietly and effectively when you are riding him, the same smooth change of pace should be possible with practice.

Throughout this transition of pace you must learn to sit quietly and maintain your correct position. Unless you do the horse will

To change from a walk to a trot, sit firmly down in the saddle and squeeze with the lower part of the legs, slightly behind the girth. Shorten the reins to bring your pony well up to the bit and continue to squeeze with the legs to maintain impulsion.

only get flustered and will not be in a position or a frame of mind to listen and respond to his rider's signals.

It is of course important to make sure your horse is in a suitable frame of mind before asking him to carry out any manoeuvre which requires concentration, whether it be show jumping, dressage, or tackling a cross-country course. There is no point in asking a horse to listen if he is too 'fresh'. Far better to allow him to 'let off steam' and then try again. If a horse is tired or unfit it is equally stupid to expect him to have his mind on his work and be able to respond quickly to your demands.

It is always more difficult to persuade a horse to change

Once he is trotting ease the reins but keep light contact with his mouth for complete control. Be very careful to keep the pressure even and don't jab at his mouth as he moves.

To move from a trot to a canter, sit down into the saddle, keeping the back straight, and squeeze with your legs just behind the girth. Sit down to a canter and keep a firm grip with your thighs so you don't bump about.

from a fast pace to a slower one, than it is, for example, to change from a trot to a canter. If you are cantering and you wish your horse to trot, this should be achieved without any direct pull on the reins. The reason is simple. If you pull on the reins, the horse's natural reaction is to pull against you. This will result in a tug-of-war action until the horse eventually slows to a trot, and to the onlooker the whole process will appear very untidy and disjointed.

If, however, you apply gentle but firm pressure with both legs and create extra energy from your horse's hindlegs, and at the same time sit down in the saddle and close your fingers so that you resist through the reins the energy you have created, your horse will almost certainly give in to this resistance and change pace smoothly and without fuss. The three pictures opposite show a smooth change of pace from a canter to a trot and finally to a walk. If you start pulling against your horse you will without doubt lose the battle, and either way your horse's natural balance will be lost.

Remember once again that your horse's hindquarters control both the rate that he slows down, and the rate that he goes faster, because they provide the power, and your hands, through the bit, provide the guidance.

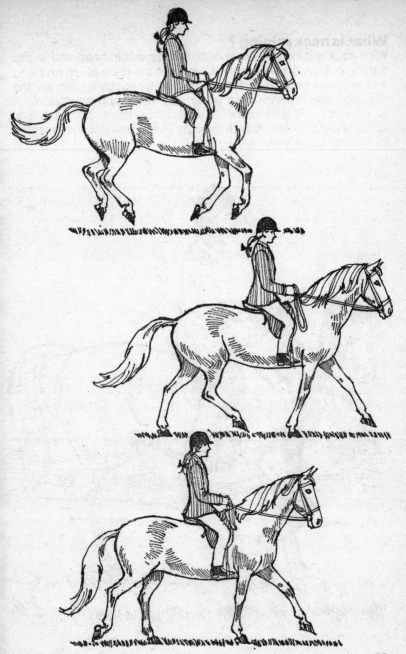

What is neck reining?

With neck reining the horse is taught by voice, hand and leg to turn away from the side on which he feels the rein against his neck, and you can encourage him to do this by touching him on the opposite side with your leg every time you want him to turn. A horse which will neck rein is certainly a very handy horse to have, and this is particularly true in the case of a horse which is expected to respond quickly and with particular agility, as in polo. (See also plate 4.)

What are the main things to remember when schooling a horse?

One of the main problems in riding is to ensure that the horse fully understands the instructions given by its rider. Quite obviously the more simple and clear the instructions, the easier it will be for the horse. For that reason it is important that you should never muddle up your aids, and be clear in your own mind exactly what you are asking the horse to do.

Never spend too long on any one lesson, and as soon as your horse has carried out your instruction correctly, make a fuss of him, and give him some tit-bit as a reward, such as a piece of carrot or apple or the occasional peppermint. It's sometimes quite amazing how quickly a horse will learn to be obedient if he knows there is a peppermint in the offing.

After he has completed his lesson correctly, return him to the stable, or let him do something he really enjoys doing, like taking

him for an interesting hack, or letting him pop over a few jumps to give him a fresh interest in the events of the day.

Rewards, and of course punishments, are particularly meaningful to a horse, and the longer you spend with horses the more you will realise the value of patience, kindness and rewards. This does not mean that you have to be soft with your horse, or let him get away with playing you up. Firmness is essential, and if he continually misbehaves, a good hard slap with the stick just behind the girth will teach him to pay attention. Never punish a horse by hitting him in front of the saddle, and *never ever* hit him on the head.

But if you are going to use your stick you must learn the art of changing it over from hand to hand, so that you will be able to give your horse a slap on either side. The reason for this is easy to understand. There is little point if a horse has swerved to the left at a fence in using your stick on his right side when you present

him again at the fence. If you do he will probably swerve to the left again. You must use the stick on his left.

Always remember, however, that the stick is no substitute for keeping your hands down in the correct position and using your legs. You will develop into a much better horseman in the long run.

Some horses develop bad habits but most of them can be eradicated by the proper use of the aids. One of the most common faults in a horse is shying, which is usually a case of nerves, or because he has seen something that reminds him of an incident he did not like or one which frightened him. You have probably noticed that a horse when he is shying never turns his head away from the object. He stares at it, and wonders what it can be, and what he should do about it.

The horse must obviously be turned from the offending object by means of the rider's hand and leg, and at the same time he must be driven forward. It is the hands and legs which will get the

horse past the object, not the stick. Hitting a horse will only make him more frightened so that he will most likely shy again.

If your horse tries to rear for any reason, it is quite wrong to think that hitting him over the head will provide the answer. You must get your weight as far forward as possible, even clasping him round the neck, and urge him forward with legs and voice. It will be a very clever horse that can walk far on his hindlegs!

A horse should never be schooled for more than ten minutes at a time. Subjecting him to longer periods will only lead to apathy or revolt, and remember that the moment you lose patience, and lose your temper, you will have lost the day.

Before blaming your horse for doing something wrong, think carefully. Did you give him the correct aids that he could readily understand, or were you asking him to do something beyond his physical or mental capabilities?

Horses, like young children, are particularly sensitive to injustice, and if you are going to reprimand your horse do it quickly

while he knows what it is for, and never overdo it. You will only lose your horse's trust and respect. Think why he may have misbehaved. A buck, for example, need not mean resistance. It can mean just that he is happy and enjoying life, or be a reminder to you that he is getting too much corn and not enough exercise.

However, you should never let your horse get into the habit of bucking. As a horse always lowers his head to buck, it is important to keep his head raised and drive him forward. If you remember to sit tight, keep your horse's head up, and push him on with your legs, you will learn to 'sit a buck' quite easily without getting flustered, and there will be less cause for alarm when your horse feels a little too fresh.

Opposite: Riding a circle is an excellent exercise for suppling your pony's back. Change the direction regularly to prevent him from becoming bored. The diameter should be 10 metres for trotting and 20 metres for cantering.

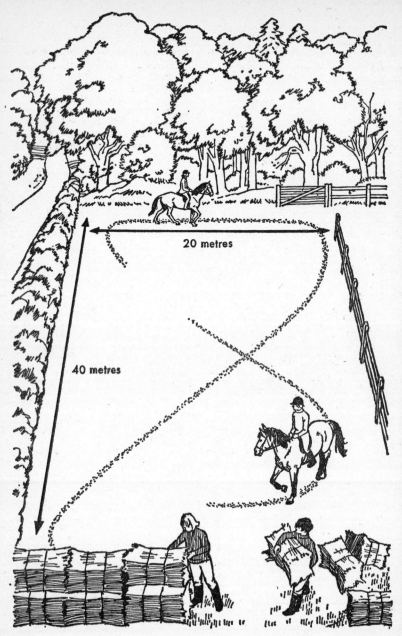

20 metres

40 metres

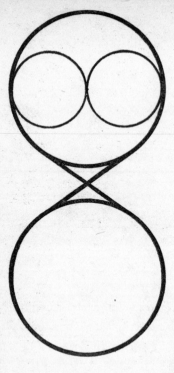

After circling you should try serpentines, loops and figures of eight. The diagrams on this page show some of the figures you can make in the schooling ring or manège illustrated opposite. Make the manège taking advantage of hedges or fences in the corner of your field and use straw bales or ropes and posts to mark the other sides.

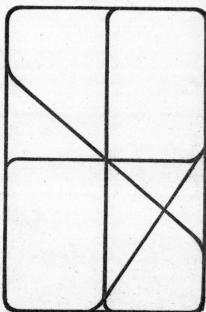

Walking and trotting over poles is a good
exercise for the beginning of a schooling period.
The poles should be placed on the ground about
1m 50cm apart. When confidence has been
established you can raise them up on bricks
(about 8 cm high) and use the same routine.

Basic dressage

What is the purpose of dressage?

Dressage is an old French term which has been adopted into the riding vocabulary, particularly in connection with the obedience phases of One Day and Three Day Events.

The object of dressage has changed considerably since it was first used for military purposes. When cavalry played an essential role in war-time, and hand-to-hand fighting was the order of the day, horses had to be taught to be handy and supple so that they could turn quickly, and gain an essential advantage for their riders by catching their opponents off balance.

The methods of dressage have, of course, changed over the

years, and the official International Equestrian Organisation, known as the Fédération Equestre Internationale, now defines the objects of dressage as:

The harmonious development of the physique and ability of the horse. As a result it makes the horse calm, supple and keen, thus achieving perfect understanding with its rider.

These qualities are revealed by: the freedom and regularity of the paces; the harmony, lightness and ease of movements; the lightening of the forehand and the engagement of the hindquarters; the horse remaining absolutely straight in any movement along a straight line and bending accordingly when moving on curved lines.

The horse thus gives the impression of doing of his own accord what is required of him.

Confident and attentive, he submits generously to the control of his rider.

His walk is regular, free and unconstrained. His trot is free, supple, regular, sustained and active. His canter is united, light and cadenced. His quarters are never inactive or sluggish. They respond to the slightest indication of the rider, and thereby give lift and spirit to the rest of his body.

By virtue of a lively impulsion and the suppleness of his joints, free from the paralysing effects of resistance, the horse obeys willingly and without hesitation, and responds to the various aids calmly and with precision.

In all his work, even at the halt, the horse must be on the bit. A horse is said to be on the bit when the hocks are correctly placed, the neck is more or less raised according to the extension or collection of the pace, the head remains steadily in position, the contact with the mouth is light, and no resistance is offered to the rider.

That may seem a rather complicated answer but it does explain exactly what judges will be looking for in a dressage test, and why dressage is important in the schooling of the horse and rider if they are going to get the most out of each other's company and effort.

Dressage is a most interesting and fascinating facet of horsemanship, particularly for those who are prepared to devote the necessary patience and perseverance to their riding. There is no mystery about dressage and every horse can be taught the rudiments.

In simple terms, in dressage we are looking for suppleness, and obedience from our horse when we tell him our intentions in clear and definite signals which he has been taught to understand.

Remember that dressage is just a natural development of confidence and harmony between horse and rider.

What is balance?

To understand balance it must be remembered that when a horse's forefeet are touching the ground they cannot be much further forward than the point of his nose. This means that if you want to

Compare this illustration with the one opposite and note particularly the position of the horse's head when the reins are being correctly applied and not allowing the horse to be off the bit as above.

lengthen a horse's stride, you must allow the head and neck to be extended.

A horse is balanced when his weight and that of the rider is distributed to allow him the maximum ease and efficiency of movement. A foal running free in a field learns to balance himself, but later, when he is broken in and taught to carry a rider, this balance will be upset because of the additional weight he will now have to carry.

Balance is achieved through exercise which develops the horse's muscles, and those of the back and hindlegs in particular. By carrying out various exercises such as moving off and stopping, altering pace, circling, turning, and eventually jumping, the rider will be able gradually to develop a good balance for his horse.

Here the horse is on the bit.

What is collection and why is it important?

A horse is said to be 'collected' when he has the maximum control over his limbs and is in a position to obey instantly any command, however slight, that is given him by his rider.

The horse needs to be hard and fit, with good strong muscles, because of the additional strain placed on the hindquarters. A horse can only become 'collected' by the sympathetic use of the hands in co-ordination with the legs and seat.

Before advanced movements can be carried out correctly, you and your horse must fully understand what collection means, and he must be able to come up to what is known as a state of collection. Let us consider the official definition of collection put forward by the British Horse Society.

The Society says: 'Collection is the concentration of the horse's energy, when the whole of his body is collected into a shortened form with a relaxed jaw on a very light rein, with even more active hindlegs, so that he has the maximum control of his limbs, and is able to obey instantly the slightest indication of his rider.'

The main thing to remember is the need for your horse to be in a position to have maximum control of his limbs so that he can quickly do what you ask of him.

How to achieve this is important. Many riders make the mistake of trying to get their horses collected by pulling back with their hands, which will usually have just the opposite results. As collection depends on the concentration of a horse's energy, and the horse develops his power or driving force from his hindquarters, it is obviously necessary to drive him forwards with your legs which control the area behind the saddle. His hindquarters then provide his support, and his head and neck, which you control through your hands, work rather like his balancing pole. The picture on page 49 and plate 2 show collected horses.

In other words, the power produced by your horse's hindquarters is brought into action by your legs and the energy generated is guided and controlled by the sympathetic use of your hands.

What is meant by being on the wrong leg?

A horse should always canter 'true' or 'united' — that is, when the leading foreleg and the leading hindleg appear to be on the same side. A horse is looked upon as cantering 'disunited' when the leading foreleg and the leading hindleg appear to be on opposite sides.

When a horse is referred to as being 'on the wrong leg' it is because he is cantering to the left with the off-foreleg leading, or to the right with the near-foreleg leading. Another term used to express the same situation is 'cantering false'.

Cantering 'united'

Cantering 'disunited'

What is counter-cantering?

Counter-cantering is carried out as an exercise to prove the horse's suppleness and obedience, by asking him to lead with the outside leg on a circle as in the pictures below.

What are the aids for cantering on a named leg?

If you want your horse to canter with the off-fore leading, which is also referred to as 'right canter', flex your horse slightly to the right with the right rein, sit well down in the saddle, and using both legs, with the left leg farther back than the right, squeeze your horse into a canter.

To canter on the 'left canter' or with the near-fore leading, flex your horse slightly to the left with the left rein and squeeze your horse into a canter with the right leg further back behind the girth

than the left. The pictures on page 53 and above show the sequence of the 'left canter'.

The reason why a horse is persuaded to canter 'united' or with the correct leg leading is to make it easier for horse and rider to maintain balance and rhythm.

How would you correct a horse cantering on the wrong leg?

If your horse canters 'disunited' or on the 'wrong leg' it is important first of all to return to a trot, and then again give him the correct aids. This must be repeated until he strikes off on the correct leg.

Never look down to see which leg your horse is leading with. With practice you will be able to feel which leg your horse is on while still maintaining your correct position in the saddle.

How would you make your horse turn on the forehand?

If you want your horse to turn to the right on the forehand from the halt, you must first of all prevent him from moving forward by means of a firm feeling on the bit and at the same time indicate to him through additional pressure on the right rein that you want him to bend his head very slightly to the right.

Keeping the weight of your body central, apply your right leg behind the girth so as to move your horse's quarters to the left. While you are doing this your left leg should be kept close to the girth to prevent him from moving backwards.

The off-fore will then be the pivoting leg, and the right hindleg should cross in front of the left hindleg. As soon as your horse has taken the necessary number of steps you should ask him to move forward without pause.

To turn to the left on the forehand the opposite aids should be given.

How would you perform a shoulder-in movement?

If a horse is not completely supple he will never become truly collected, and so it is important to know not only how to encourage suppleness, but also how it can be maintained.

Remember that the more supple you can make your horse, the more obedient he will become, and the shoulder-in exercise is particularly designed to supple a horse's body.

The use of a wall or covered school is very helpful in performing the shoulder-in. Let us consider the left shoulder-in and use the corner of the covered school as our starting point. As you ride through the corner to the left, ask with your left rein as though you were going to circle to the left. The right rein should also be used, however, to prevent your horse from completing the circle, with your left leg pressing at the girth, and your right leg placed slightly behind the girth.

The hindquarters of your horse must now be kept on their original track, and you must encourage him to move forward along the wall with his right shoulder leading his left hip, and his left shoulder moving to the outside of his left hip.

This exercise should be taken in slow but definite stages. It can produce suppleness of body and a longer stride from the hindlegs and this can prove to be particularly useful, for example when jumping.

How would you ask a horse to lengthen his stride?

If you wish to improve your horse's paces you must ask him to lengthen his stride so that more ground can be covered with a minimum of additional effort. This is particularly useful in jumping when you can regulate the length of your horse's stride so that he arrives at the correct take-off point for his fences.

In asking your horse to extend you are, of course, requiring him to lengthen not only his stride but also his whole form. For him to do this you must allow him to maintain his balance by lowering his head and extending his neck. The same applies whether you

A collected stride

are asking for an extended trot or an extended canter.

First encourage your horse to move forward with greater energy but not more quickly. By closing your legs on your horse and 'squeezing' him forward you can also use your seat to ask for greater impulsion. Keep a light contact on your horse's mouth, but give him enough rein so that he has freedom to use his head and neck to maintain balance. Your body should be slightly further forward in the extended paces than is usual in the collected gaits, so that you can maintain the correct rhythm.

An extended stride

How should the rein back be performed?

The rein back is a movement which is frequently performed incorrectly because people forget that it is really more of a forward movement.

Make sure that your horse has a relaxed jaw, and is standing squarely. Then ask him to move forward in the normal way by squeezing your legs. At the same time, prevent him from moving forward by a steady pressure on the reins. Instead of going forward, your horse will act against the resistance provided by your hands, and move steadily backwards, his legs moving in diagonals. The pictures show the action.

Your horse should rein back in a straight line, and any movement to the left or right should be corrected by your legs in the usual way. Never try to pull your horse backwards. It will only result in resistance on his part.

Going for a ride

What should you do first ?

Before setting out on a ride always make sure that your horse is properly saddled and bridled, that all your tack is in good condition and that the horse's shoes are tight and in good order. (See plate 5.)

Do this yourself. Never leave it to anyone else. You are going to be riding the horse and it is your comfort and safety that is at stake.

You will no doubt have read of jockeys losing races because of a broken stirrup leather or a slipping saddle. How the trainers and jockeys concerned must have wished that they had taken that little bit of extra trouble and checked more carefully that everything was all right. A curb chain that has not been twisted correctly until it lies flat will give pain to your horse and cause him to resist your instructions. A saddle put on in too much haste, with the

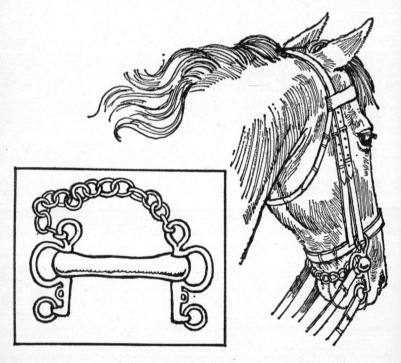

bottom of the panel folded over, can cause a saddle sore that may prevent your horse from being ridden for days if not weeks.

When you clean your tack be sure to check all the stitching, but when you go to saddle up always make certain that your bridle has not only been put back together correctly, but that the various pieces have been assembled in their correct holes.

Having made certain that your horse is happy and all his saddlery is correct, it will be time to mount up and face the events of the ride with the assurance that at least you won't have any problems with your tack.

How should you set off and return?

There is a very good saying that when you go for a ride you should always walk the first mile out and the last mile back. Doing so makes a lot of good common sense.

When you set off give your horse time to settle down and become accustomed to your weight in the saddle. Don't lounge in the saddle. A fresh horse may shy and if you are riding like a sack of potatoes you may soon be off. It also looks slovenly and it shows bad horsemanship. Sit straight and keep your horse up into his bridle by the impulsion of your legs.

As you come to the end of the ride, slacken the girths and walk your horse for the last three-quarters of a mile. Then dismount and lead him for the last quarter mile to make sure that he is cool by the time you arrive at the stable. If he is still hot when you arrive, put on a sweat rug and lead him out until he has cooled off.

How can you make sure that you and your horse both enjoy the ride?

First of all, try to choose a different route each day. Like humans, horses become bored, and if you continually ride your horse along the same route, he will get to know every twist and turn and become weary of the whole thing.

If you have to exercise two horses at the same time, make sure you ride each of them on alternate days. There is no excuse for riding the same horse each day and leading the other even though one of them may be your favourite.

Never lead a horse in a headcollar. Make sure the horse you are leading has a proper bridle and always lead on the left (in countries where traffic is driven on the left) keeping yourself between the led horse and the traffic. If the horse you are leading has a snaffle bridle, pull the near-side rein under his chin and through the off-side ring of the bit and this will give you a decent length of rein to hold. If you are going to exercise two horses regularly, it is as well to buy a leading-rein with two clip fasteners which should be attached to the rings of the snaffle.

Steady slow roadwork is good for hardening your horse's legs and building up muscle. It will also get him used to heavy traffic and other road noises.

If your horse is nervous in traffic do not go out on the road alone. The main danger will be the possibility of traffic brushing

past you, and this can be particularly dangerous if your horse shies or becomes frightened at something in a hedge. If he is liable to shy at heavy vehicles or tractors, it is less likely that he will do so in the company of other horses, particularly if they are older and more experienced. They will be able to give you a lead and he will be able to see that these 'monsters' are really quite harmless after all. Make sure that the rider with the quietest horse that is traffic-proof rides on your outside nearest the traffic.

Horses enjoy a good canter. You only have to watch them at a Horse Show, and you will see them prick their ears when the order is given to 'canter on'. How they love to crack their nostrils,

and throw up their heads in excitement after they have had a good 'pipe opener'. If the going is good and other conditions are right, cantering work, providing it is not overdone, is good for the lungs and helps to clear the wind.

However, you must remember that a horse which is probably docile on the road may become quite another type of animal when he feels the turf under his feet. Perhaps his previous owner let him have his head as soon as he reached a stretch of grass and so your horse may automatically want to gallop. Restrain him until you can regulate the pace, and if he stiffens his neck, or 'swallows a poker' as some old grooms used to call it, keep cool and try to bring him round into a circle. Never punish him, because he won't understand why you are doing so. Talk to him and soothe him, then take him back to the place where he started to gallop.

Try and settle him down, but if he sets off hell for leather again, bring him round in a circle and start all over again. He will eventually realise that being on grass is not necessarily a signal to gallop, and become more amenable to your own wishes.

A horse which is inclined to run away can also be stopped by slight and alternate pulls on the reins, but never maintain a steady pull on the horse's mouth. This will only deaden it and make him resist your action. Horses can be annoying at times, but patience and understanding can do more good than any amount of shouting and hitting. A thoughtless or a hasty act can undo months of careful training, and the establishment of that link of confidence and trust which is so necessary between horse and rider. Remember that some horses, just like people, are less intelligent than others, and they take longer to grasp what is being asked of them, and the immediate significance of the various aids.

It is not necessary to gallop a horse more than once or twice a week in order to keep him fit and happy, and when you do it is a good idea to find a slight rise which will not only help to develop his muscle, but will also make him easier to stop.

If you try to vary your ride each day, this may mean negotiating some steep hills. Horses as a rule are much more clever at going downhill than uphill. Their inherent instinct warns them to walk downhill, and if it is very steep they will often slide down on their own accord, ears pricked, and carefully picking out the best way.

Sit down in the saddle with your body slightly forward and your weight over the horse's centre of gravity. Your leg pressure should be maintained to ensure that your horse's hindquarters don't slip sideways. Leave his mouth alone as much as possible, but always ride straight down a hill or steep slope, and never try to zigzag down.

When going uphill the horse's natural inclination is to try and canter up to the top. You must, however, restrain him. Sit forward in the saddle and allow your horse to use his neck as a sort of balancing pole, as in the picture above. Just sit still. He will need little guidance.

Horses are gregarious animals who appreciate company, and as they usually go much better in the company of others, it is always a good idea to try and ensure that you ride out with someone else as frequently as possible. You must, of course, make sure your horse will be prepared to behave properly when he is alone, or when other horses go off in a different direction, so give him practice by hacking alone and in company.

How should you behave?

Whether you are alone or with others, you should always ride with consideration for other people, and other road users, and when drivers slow down for you give them a smile and a wave of thanks. Many motorists think horsemen and women are a 'stuck-up' bunch of people. It is up to you to show them they are wrong.

Don't canter along the grass verges by the side of the road. Your horse may be startled by something and shy into the road in front of traffic, and there is always the danger that there may be broken glass or some other piece of rubbish which could cut and lame your horse and which you may not see until too late.

If you have not already done so, it would be a good idea to get copies of *The Safety Code for Riding* and *Ride Safely* issued by the British Horse Society, and make sure you are fully conversant with the Highway Code.

Although steady roadwork will help to muscle up your horse, make sure that you keep off the roads when the traffic is likely to be heavy. Keeping lines of cars and lorries waiting to pass will not endear you to other road users, and it won't be much fun for your horse either.

It is important that all bridle paths should be ridden as frequently as possible in order to ensure that they are kept open. Perhaps you will be lucky enough to persuade local farmers to give you permission to ride round their fields along the headlands. If they do, make sure you do not abuse their friendship. Always shut gates; never leave paper around; and make sure that you do not disturb their stock more than you have to through your presence there. Never ride over growing crops or clover or seeds, and don't gallop over grassland, cutting up the turf, if it is wet.

If a suitable opportunity arises to put your horse over a jump, it will help keep his interest, but make sure you will not be trespassing or doing any damage to other people's property. It is also wise to make certain, if you jump over a fence into a field or bridleway, that there is room to jump back again if you need to do so.

How should you open a gate?

Every rider should know the correct way of opening a gate on horseback. Having to get off every time you meet a gate when out riding is not only a nuisance, it is also an indication of poor horsemanship.

To open the gate ride the horse parallel to the gate from the hinge end towards the latch. Open the latch with the hand nearest the gate. Pass through, turn the horse round and push or pull the gate to. Make the horse stand parallel and close to the gate, while you lean down to fix the latch with the hand nearest the latch, having previously transferred the whip and reins to the other hand. Plate 8 shows a well-trained pony allowing his rider to open a gate.

If you are riding with other people, make sure that the gate is securely fastened before anyone rides off. It is not only good manners, it is important from the point of view of safety, because the rider shutting the gate may otherwise have difficulty in controlling his horse and the reins could get caught in the latch.

The correct dress

What should you wear for hacking?

Because of the substantial increases in price of all riding wear in recent years, there has been some relaxation in the standard of dress worn for everyday hacking and riding. This is a pity because a handsome and well turned out horse or pony deserves a rider looking smart and efficient, and if you can afford to do so you should always dress properly when you take your horse out on the road. You can always change back into an old sweater and slacks or jeans on your return when you have to tackle the stable chores.

There are three main essentials as far as dress is concerned every time you get on a horse, whether you are exercising on the roads or schooling in the field. These are the following: you must wear a hard hat; you must wear a boot or shoe with a proper heel; and you must ensure that your clothing is comfortable and not too tight to restrict your movement. These three things are essential for safety reasons. (See plate 10.)

If you want to be correct, however, you should always wear a hard hat in the form of a velvet cap or riding bowler; a riding jacket; a shirt with a collar and tie; a waistcoat or pullover if it is cold; jodhpurs and jodhpur boots or breeches and riding boots.

What should you wear when hunting?

Most Hunts encourage young riders, and providing you and your horse always look neat and tidy, it is unlikely that the Secretary will have cause to complain. It is a formal occasion, however, and you must be specially careful with your own and your pony's appearance.

A riding jacket or 'ratcatcher' will be quite adequate worn over a shirt with a collar and tie, and it will also be permissible to wear jodhpurs and jodhpur boots, or breeches with black riding boots. If you wear boots, however, you must also wear spurs. As far as headgear is concerned, girls and young boys may wear a black velvet riding cap or a bowler. Whenever you wear a velvet cap out hunting, however, you must make sure that the tabs at the back of the hat are either cut off or sewn up inside so that they don't show. Plate 11 shows a young rider correctly dressed.

Gloves may also be worn and you must have a hunting whip with a thong and lash. Apart from being smart, the gloves will be useful if your reins become slippery either through rain or from the sweat on your horse's neck, and it is useful to keep a spare pair under your saddle held in place by the girth. The hunting whip is not to crack at hounds, but to use to keep them away from your horse's legs. The handle will also be helpful in opening gates.

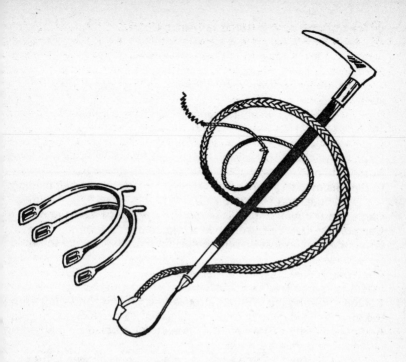

When you reach the age of eighteen you will be expected to wear more formal dress. This consists of a shirt with a white stock or hunting tie; buff coloured riding breeches and black riding boots with spurs; a black or blue riding jacket or fully skirted black hunting coat; and a top hat in the case of a man, or a bowler or black or blue velvet cap in the case of a woman. Farmers are also allowed to wear a black velvet cap, and grooms or second horsemen may wear a bowler. Gloves must again be worn, and everyone must have a hunting whip with thong and lash.

In addition to the hunt officials, a man who is lucky enough to be given permission by the Master to wear the hunt button will be able to wear a scarlet hunting coat, but this must always be worn with a top hat. Only the Master, past Masters, hunt servants and officials of the hunt are allowed to wear a black riding cap with a scarlet hunting coat. Silk hats are never worn when hunting with a pack of staghounds, and they should not be used before the opening meet or after April 1st.

Glossary

Artificial aids   Items like sticks and spurs used by a rider to signal his intention to his horse.

Black hunting coat   Usually fully skirted and wool-lined like a short overcoat.

Breeches   Riding wear, buttoned at the knee, worn with full-length boots.

Bucking   When a horse lowers his head, arches his back, and leaps with all four feet off the ground.

Butcher boots   A type of black knee-length riding boot.

Canter disunited   When the leading foreleg and the leading hindleg appear to be on opposite sides.

Canter on   When a horse is asked to canter from a slower pace.

Cantering true   A horse is said to be cantering 'true' or 'united' when the leading foreleg and the leading hindleg appear to be on the same side.

Cantering united   When a horse canters with the correct leg leading.

Cantering wrong leg   When a horse is cantering to the left with the off-foreleg leading or to the right with the near-foreleg leading.

Centre of gravity   The centre of gravity for a horse runs along a vertical line through the withers.

Collected   When a horse has maximum control over his limbs and movements.

Dressage   An old French term used to describe various movements which help to supple a horse and make him more obedient.

Garters   Leather straps used with riding boots.

Good hands   A rider's hands which are light and responsive.

Hard mouth   A term used to describe a horse's mouth ruined by the incorrect use of a rider's hands.

Hunt button   A button, worn by members of a hunt, which has been awarded them by the Master.

Hunting whip   A whip with a thong and lash used out hunting.

Independent seat   A strong seat independent of the reins to keep a rider in the correct position in the saddle.

Jodhpurs   Riding trousers fastened usually with a zip and worn with jodhpur boots.

Jodhpur boots   Ankle-length boots worn with jodhpurs and either elastic-sided or fastened by a leather strap.

Leading rein   A strap, usually made of either leather or webbing, used to lead another horse.

Left-canter When a horse canters to the left leading with the near-foreleg.

Lungeing When a horse is exercised at the end of a lunge rein in a circle without a rider.

Mounting block A block usually made of brick or stone used for mounting a horse.

Natural aids Signals used by a rider to convey his instructions to a horse.

Neck reining When a horse has been taught by voice, hand and heel to turn away from the side on which he feels the rein on his neck.

Obedience When a horse carries out a rider's instructions without resistance.

Pipe opener A good strong gallop.

Ratcatcher A type of riding jacket.

Rearing When a horse goes up on his hindlegs.

Right canter When the off-fore leads.

Rein back When a horse moves steadily backwards at a rider's commands in response to hands and legs.

Resistance When a horse goes against a rider's instructions.

Shoulder-in A movement in dressage.

Stock A hunting neck cloth specially tied and held in place with a pin.

Shying When a horse or pony, usually through nerves, swerves away from an object.

Traffic proof When a horse is good in traffic.

Velvet cap A peaked hard riding cap.

Other horse and pony books by the same authors

Robert Owen

My Learn to Ride Book Illustrated in colour throughout, this is an informative book aimed at giving younger people an all-round introduction to horsemanship.

Successful Riding and Jumping The techniques necessary to develop the skills of riding and jumping successfully are clearly described.

John Bullock

Horse and Pony Quiz Book Specially written for horse lovers of all ages, this book gives an enormous amount of information on the care and enjoyment of the horse.

Robert Owen and John Bullock

The Horse and Pony Gift Book A big book, packed with facts about horse care and health, breeds, training, buying, the work of the farrier, gymkhanas, riding holidays, show jumping and all the equestrian sports. Illustrated throughout in black and white and colour.

Young Riders Guides

Buying and Keeping a Horse or Pony
Caring for a Horse or Pony
Riding and Schooling
About Jumping

More Beaver Books

We hope you have enjoyed this Beaver Book. Here are some of the other titles:

Merlin's Mistake Brian, Maude and Tertius (Tertius is Merlin's 'mistake' because he was given the gift of all future knowledge in error) set out on a quest which leads them through many adventures, both dangerous and funny, to an unexpected but satisfying conclusion. By Robert Newman, author of *The Twelve Labours of Hercules*, also in Beavers

My Favourite Horse Stories Dorian Williams has chosen fifteen of his favourite stories and poems about horses, by authors such as Tolstoy, Shakespeare and Dick Francis; a collection to delight all animal lovers

Amazing But True A collection of stories about amazing people, places and events, from the Man in the Iron Mask to the stone statues on Easter Island and the unsolved mystery of the *Mary Celeste;* illustrated throughout

The Crocodile Based on the true story of Mary Anning, John Tully's novel for older children is set in Lyme Regis and tells of Mary's search for fossils – especially the famous 'Crocodile' – against a background of the Napoleonic Wars. With illustrations by Clifford Bayly

White Fang Jack London's great classic story about the life of a wild wolf dog at the time of the Gold Rush in the Yukon

New Beavers are published every month and if you would like the *Beaver Bulletin* – which gives all the details – please send a large stamped addressed envelope to:

Beaver Bulletin
The Hamlyn Group
Astronaut House
Feltham
Middlesex TW14 9AR

37582X